delicious desserts

Published by:
TRIDENT PRESS INTERNATIONAL
801 12th Avenue South, Suite 400
Naples, Fl 34102 USA
Tel: + 1 239 649 7077
Fax: + 1 239 649 5832
Email: tridentpress@worldnet.att.net
Websites: www.trident-international.com
www.chefexpressinternational.com

Delicious desserts

Publishers: Simon St. John Bailey and
Elaine S. Evans
Editor-in-chief: Isabel Toyos

Texts
Editing and supervision: Aurora Giribaldi
Translation: Sandra Heyman
Proofreading: Rosa Corgatelli

Design and layout
Cover: Matilde Bossi
Inside: M&A Gráfica
Step by step photography: Fernando Giampieri
Step by step styling: Emi Pechar

Prepress
Mikonos Comunicación Gráfica

Includes Index
ISBN 158279670X
UPC 6 15269 79670 2

First Edition Printed in February 2004

Printed in Peru by Quebecor

introduction

Indulge yourself with irresistible temptations, finish the perfect meal with the perfect dessert. Whether it's a family dinner, a special birthday, a festive occasion, a dessert for supper or just because you need a treat, this book supplies most sumptuous desserts to suit any meal.

Pies and tarts

Whatever the combination of filling and pastry you choose, pies and tarts will always be a popular dessert item.
Pies served warm are commonly made with fruits such as apples, pears, and so.

delicious desserts
introduction

Fruit

Fresh fruit, whatever poached or marinated, puréed and molded or simply served with an appropriate sauce, will always have its place at dessert time. For poached fruits, always choose fruit that is firm. Maintain the liquid at a gentle simmer and let the fruit cool in it so the final product will be very flavorful.

Feuilletés

The main components for a successful feuilleté are fresh, seasonal fruit of the finest quality and puff pastry. Feuilletés are at their best when assembled just before serving.

Mousses

Mousse translates into "froth". A basic mousse usually contains eggs, cream, flavorings, and sometimes gelatin. Most often, the egg whites are made into a meringue which accounts for the light, airy texture which is characteristic of most mousses.

Puddings

Puddings have long been a very popular and traditional dessert in many countries. Bread puddings and fruit puddings, baked and even uncooked, are two basic kinds of puddings. Any number of variations are possible when preparing them.

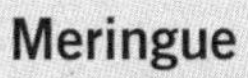

Meringue

In order to obtain a proper meringue, all utensils must be clean and dry. Be careful that no traces of fat come in contact with the egg whites. Some sort of acid, like lemon juice, is sometimes used to help the egg whites rise and remain firm. Egg whites are usually beaten on high speed and the sugar is added gradually during the process.

Soufflés

The French word soufflé means "puffed up". Avoid opening the oven door during the initial baking process, as any sudden draft could cause the soufflé to collapse. Soufflés should be presented and eaten immediately because, as the saying goes, "a soufflé waits for no one".

Crêpes

The consistency of the batter should be fairly thin so it spreads quickly and evenly when placed in a hot crêpe pan. Crêpes are usually cooked to a golden brown on one side, then turned and cooked for a few seconds on the other side. The browned side always faces up.

Fritters

Always make certain the oil is hot enough for frying before adding the fritters, otherwise, they tend to absorb too much oil resulting in a soggy product.

Difficult scale

■□□ | Easy to do

■■□ | Requires attention

■■■ | Requires experience

poached pears with chocolate ganache

■■□ | Cooking time: 20 - Preparation time: 30 minutes

ingredients

- 4 firm pears, stems intact
- 1 cup caster sugar
- 3 cups water
- 2 tablespoons freshly squeezed lemon juice
- 1 cup sweet white wine
- 3/4 cup thickened cream
- 100 g/3 1/2 oz milk chocolate

method

1. Peel pears and level off the bottoms so they will stand upright.
2. Bring sugar, water, lemon juice and wine to the boil in a large saucepan over moderate heat, reduce heat to simmer. Add the pears and poach for 15-20 minutes or until just tender. Allow pears to cool in syrup.
3. To make ganache, boil cream in a medium saucepan over moderate heat until reduced by a third. Remove from heat, add chocolate, stir until smooth; set aside to cool until thick enough to pipe.
4. Drain pears, cut the top third of each one off, pipe ganache onto pear, replace the top of the pear.

Serves 4

tip from the chef

It is important to choose very firm pears to avoid breaking during cooking.
In order to obtain colored pears, you may substitute red wine or green mint liqueur for the white wine.

chocolate
marble cheesecake

a

■□□ | Cooking time: 75 minutes - Preparation time: 15 minutes

method

1. Mix together biscuit crumbs and butter until combined, press mixture over base and sides of a 22 cm/$8\frac{3}{4}$ in springform pan (a); chill.
2. To make filling, blend or process cream cheese with caster sugar, flour, essence and eggs until smooth (b). Divide mixture into two bowls, quickly mixing the melted chocolate and cocoa into one of the bowls (c). Pour the plain mixture into the biscuit crust. Pour chocolate mixture onto plain batter and gently swirl mixture together with a spatula (d) to create a marble pattern.
3. Bake cheesecake in moderate oven for $1\frac{1}{4}$ hour; set aside to cool to room temperature. Chill cheesecake and decorate with piped cream just prior to serving.

Serves 8

ingredients

- **250 g/$\frac{1}{2}$ lb packet golden oatmeal biscuits, crushed**
- **100 g/$3\frac{1}{2}$ oz butter, melted**
- **500 g/1 lb cream cheese, softened**
- **$1\frac{1}{2}$ cups caster sugar**
- **$\frac{1}{4}$ cup plain flour**
- **$1\frac{1}{2}$ tablespoon vanilla essence**
- **5 eggs**
- **100 g/$3\frac{1}{2}$ oz milk chocolate, melted**
- **4 tablespoons cocoa**
- **$1\frac{1}{2}$ cups double cream, whipped**

tip from the chef

It is irresistible if served with raspberry sauce or lemon curd.

b

c

d

chocolate tart

■■■ | Cooking time: 35 minutes - Preparation time: 40 minutes

method

1. To make pastry, place flour, cocoa, sugar, butter, egg yolk, vinegar and iced water in a blender or food processor and process for about 10 seconds or until mixture begins to bind. Wrap in foil and chill for 30 minutes.
2. Dust working surface with cocoa, and roll out pastry to fit a 23 cm/9 in removable base flan tin, or a 23 cm/9 in ovenproof pie dish. Fill case with foil, then pastry weights. Bake in moderately hot oven for 10 minutes. Remove foil and weights and cook for a further 10 minutes. Cool completely.
3. To make filling, beat custard with electric mixer, pour in melted chocolate while motor is operating, pour in cream, add sugar, mix until combined. Dissolve gelatin in 3 tablespoons cold water, stir in double saucepan over simmering water until dissolved. Stir in custard/chocolate mixture. Pour mixture into cooled pastry shell, chill until set.
4. To make topping, melt chocolate with butter in double saucepan over simmering water. Quickly spread over the top of pie using a spatula. Decorate with chocolate leaves and icing sugar. Chill until served.

Serves 8

ingredients

pastry

- **1 cup plain flour**
- **1/4 cup sweetened cocoa powder**
- **1 tablespoon brown sugar**
- **6 tablespoons chilled butter, cut into small cubes**
- **1 egg yolk**
- **2 teaspoons white vinegar**
- **2 tablespoons iced water**

filling

- **1 cup carton custard**
- **200 g/6 1/2 oz dark chocolate, melted**
- **1 cup thickened cream**
- **3 tablespoons icing sugar**
- **2 tablespoons gelatin**

topping

- **90 g/3 oz dark chocolate**
- **1 tablespoon butter**
- **chocolate leaves and icing sugar, to decorate**

tip from the chef

Chocolate is made from the seeds of tropical cacao tree. The scientific name of the tree, the Greek term theobroma, means literally "food of the gods".

white chocolate fondue

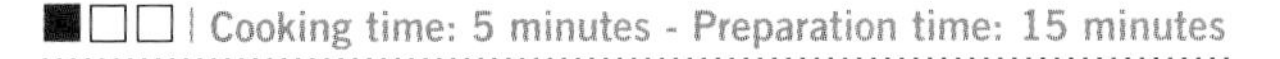
■□□ | Cooking time: 5 minutes - Preparation time: 15 minutes

method

1. Combine chocolate with cream and brandy in a medium saucepan over low heat. Stir constantly until chocolate has melted and mixture is smooth. Pour mixture into a medium bowl and set aside to cool to room temperature.
2. Cut wooden skewers in half, discard bottom halves. Thread a piece of strawberry, marshmallow and a grape onto each skewer, serve with dipping sauce.

Serves 8

ingredients

- **250 g/1/2 lb white chocolate, chopped**
- **3/4 cup thickened cream**
- **1 tablespoon brandy**
- **1 small box strawberries, hulled and quartered**
- **1 cup marshmallows, halved**
- **1 cup green seedless grapes**

tip from the chef

If you wish, you may add 1/2 spoon of grated coconut, and replace the brandy by 2 tablespoons of rum.
It is important to cut the fruit at the last moment to avoid oxidation.

mandarin cointreau cake

■■■ | Cooking time: 40 minutes - Preparation time: 20 minutes

ingredients

- 4 eggs
- 3/4 cup caster sugar
- 2 tablespoons plain flour
- 1/3 cup self-raising flour
- 1/2 cup custard powder
- 1/3 cup ground almonds
- 2 tablespoons finely grated mandarin rind

filling

- 3 egg yolks
- 1/2 cup caster sugar
- 3 tablespoons cornflour
- 2 tablespoons Cointreau
- 1 cup evaporated milk
- 1/3 cup double cream, whipped
- 3/4 cup melted apricot jam

topping

- 1 cup double cream, whipped
- 3/4 cup canned mandarin segments, drained

method

1. Beat eggs with an electric mixer until thick. Gradually add sugar and beat for a further 3 minutes. Fold in combined plain flour, self-raising flour, custard powder, almonds and rind. Pour mixture into a greased and lined 22 cm/8 3/4 in round cake pan and bake in moderate oven for 30 minutes. Turn onto a wire rack, cool completely.
2. To make filling, combine egg yolks, caster sugar, cornflour and Cointreau in a medium saucepan, gradually stir in evaporated milk, stir until filling boils and thickens. Cool to room temperature, stir in whipped cream until combined.
3. Cut cake into 3 layers. Spread layers with apricot jam, then sandwich with filling and cover sides and top of cake with whipped cream. Decorate with mandarin segments.

Serves 8

tip from the chef

Cointreau is an orange liqueur created in 1849 in Angers, France, by Adolphe Cointreau and his brother. In this recipe it may be replaced by any other orange or mandarin liqueur.

lemon chiffon pie

■■■ | Cooking time: 2 minutes - Preparation time: 20 minutes

method

1. Blend or process biscuits until they resemble fine crumbs. Mix with butter and press into a 22 cm/8 3/4 in springform pan, pressing crumbs as far up the sides as possible.
2. Beat egg yolks with sugar and lemon rind until light and fluffy. Heat lemon juice over high heat until boiling, slowly pour into egg mixture in a thin steady stream while motor is operating. Dissolve gelatin in wine in a double saucepan over simmering water; stir into egg mixture.
3. Beat egg whites until stiff, gradually add extra sugar and beat for a further 3 minutes. Fold into egg/lemon mixture and pour into biscuit case.
4. Refrigerate to set. Decorate with lemon slices.

Serves 6

ingredients

- **250 g/8 oz golden oatmeal biscuits**
- **75 g/2 1/2 oz butter, melted**
- **4 eggs, separated**
- **grated rind of 1 lemon**
- **1/2 cup caster sugar**
- **1/2 cup freshly squeezed lemon juice**
- **2 teaspoons gelatin**
- **1/4 cup white wine**
- **1/4 cup caster sugar, extra**
- **lemon slices**

tip from the chef

When grating lemon, only the yellow rind should be included, as the white pith would add a bitter taste to the dessert.

orange terrine

■□□ | Cooking time: 3 minutes - Preparation time: 25 minutes

ingredients

- > $2^1/_2$ sachets gelatin
- > 3 cups apple juice
- > 2 tablespoons freshly squeezed lemon juice
- > 2 teaspoons freshly squeezed lime juice
- > 1 tablespoon freshly chopped mint
- > 2 oranges, peeled and segmented
- > $1^1/_2$ cups freshly squeezed orange juice
- > 2 tablespoons Cointreau
- > 2 tablespoons grated orange rind

method

1. Stir gelatin in $^3/_4$ cup water in a double saucepan over simmering water until crystals have dissolved.
2. Divide apple juice into two separate bowls. In the first bowl combine apple juice with $^1/_3$ of gelatin, lemon juice, lime juice and mint. Lightly oil a loaf pan, about 4-cup capacity, and gently pour the minted apple mixture into the pan. Chill for several hours or until set.
3. To make orange layer, arrange orange segments in a row along the top of the already set jelly. Combine orange juice with the Cointreau and $^1/_3$ of gelatin and gently pour over the back of a spoon, over the orange segments in order not to disturb the already set jelly. Chill for seven hours or until set.
4. Combine remaining apple juice with orange rind and remaining gelatin and gently pour over the set orange jelly. Chill until firm. Ease jelly out and serve with cream.

Serves 6

tip from the chef

It is a very simple and fresh dessert. The fruity note makes it ideal for Summer days.

mango mold with raspberry coulis

■□□ | Cooking time: 2 minutes - Preparation time: 20 minutes

ingredients

- 1 cup chopped fresh mango
- 1 tablespoon freshly squeezed lemon juice
- 1/4 cup apricot nectar
- 1 tablespoon Cointreau
- 1 tablespoon gelatin
- 1/2 cup double cream, whipped
- 1 small box raspberries
- 2 tablespoons raspberry jam
- 2 tablespoons freshly squeezed orange juice
- 2 tablespoons Framboise
- 1 mango, peeled, stoned and chopped, to garnish

method

1. Blend or process mango pulp with lemon juice, apricot nectar and Cointreau, until smooth (a).
2. Dissolve gelatin in cold water, stir over a double saucepan of simmering water until clear. Stir into mango mixture, fold in cream (b), until combined.
3. Pour mixture into 4, lightly greased, 1/2-cup capacity molds (c), chill to set.
4. Blend or process raspberries with jam, orange juice and Framboise until smooth. Strain coulis through a sieve (d) and discard pips.
5. Unmold mango mousse and serve with raspberry coulis and fresh mango pieces.

Serves 4

tip from the chef

The mango is original from India, where it is considered the king of fruits.
Raspberries may be replaced by peeled mandarin segments.

a

b

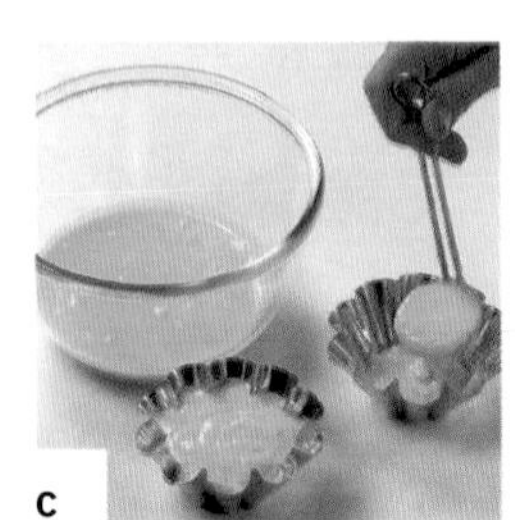
c

d

dark chocolate bavarois

■■□ | Cooking time: 15 minutes - Preparation time: 20 minutes

method

1. Beat egg yolks with sugar until light and creamy. Slowly bring milk to the boil, pour over egg mixture while motor is operating. Return mixture to saucepan over low heat, stir constantly until mixture thickens slightly, about 3 minutes.
2. Dissolve gelatin in 1/4 cup water over double saucepan. Remove custard from heat, stir in gelatin and melted chocolate. Cool for 10 minutes.
3. Beat cream until soft peaks form, fold into chocolate mixture. Lightly grease four 1-cup capacity molds, pour in mousse and refrigerate until set.
4. To make sauce, combine chocolate and extra cream in a medium saucepan, stir over low heat until combined. Cool to room temperature. Ease bavarois out of molds and pour sauce over the top.

Serves 4

ingredients

> **4 egg yolks**
> **1/4 cup caster sugar**
> **1 cup milk**
> **2 teaspoons gelatin**
> **200 g/6 1/2 oz dark chocolate, melted**
> **1 cup thickened cream**

sauce

> **100 g/3 1/2 oz white chocolate, grated**
> **3/4 cup thickened cream, extra**

tip from the chef

In step 1, it is important not to let the egg yolk and milk mixture boil, as it would curdle. If the mixture happens to boil in spite of the care taken, it may be saved by blending it for a couple of seconds.

layered fruit terrine

■■□ | Cooking time: 5 minutes - Preparation time: 25 minutes

ingredients

- 1 star fruit (carambola), sliced
- 1 peach, peeled, stoned and sliced

mango layer

- 1 cup/250 ml/8 fl oz mango purée
- 2 tablespoons caster sugar
- 2 tablespoons Cointreau
- 4 teaspoons gelatin dissolved in $^1/_3$ cup/90 ml/3 fl oz hot water, cooled
- $^3/_4$ cup/185 ml/6 fl oz double cream, whipped

passion fruit layer

- $^1/_2$ cup/125 ml/4 fl oz passion fruit pulp
- 2 tablespoons orange juice
- 2 tablespoons caster sugar
- 2 tablespoons Midori (melon liqueur)
- 4 teaspoons gelatin dissolved in $^1/_3$ cup/90 ml/3 fl oz hot water, cooled
- $^3/_4$ cup/185 ml/6 oz double cream, whipped

method

1. Arrange slices of star fruit over base and sides of a lightly oiled glass or ceramic 9 x 23 cm/3$^1/_2$ x 9$^1/_2$ in loaf dish.
2. To make mango layer, combine mango purée, sugar and Cointreau in a large bowl. Stir in gelatin mixture and fold in cream. Pour carefully over fruit in loaf dish and refrigerate until firm.
3. To make passion fruit layer, combine passion fruit pulp, orange juice, sugar and Midori in a large bowl. Stir in gelatin mixture and fold in cream.
4. Place a layer of peach slices over set mango layer, then carefully top with passion fruit mixture and refrigerate until set. To serve, unmold terrine and cut into slices.

Serves 10

tip from the chef

Layers of Summer fruit set in tropical-flavored mousse are an ideal dessert when feeding a crowd. Run a spatula around the edge of the terrine to free it from the sides of the dish, before turning out.

passion fruit mousse

■□□ | Cooking time: 2 minutes - Preparation time: 15 minutes

method

1. Scoop out passion fruit pulp into a medium bowl. Dissolve gelatin in orange juice in double saucepan over simmering water. Add to the passion fruit, mix well.
2. Beat cream until thick and gently fold into purée mixture. Spoon mousse into 4 glasses, chill to serve. Decorate with passion fruit seed.

Serves 4

ingredients

- **10 passion fruits**
- **2 teaspoons gelatin**
- **1/4 cup freshly squeezed orange juice**
- **1 1/2 cup thickened cream**

tip from the chef

It is a quick and easy dessert, very handy for busy cooks.

double chocolate velvet mousse

■□□ | Cooking time: 0 minute - Preparation time: 25 minutes

ingredients

- 200 g/6 1/2 oz milk chocolate melts
- 1 cup sour cream
- 2 egg yolks
- 4 egg whites
- 1/4 cup caster sugar
- 200 g/6 1/2 oz white chocolate melts
- 1/2 cup cream, whipped, to decorate
- 4 strawberries, to decorate
- 1 tablespoon sifted cocoa, to decorate

method

1. Combine milk chocolate melts with half the sour cream and 1 egg yolk in a large bowl, stir until smooth. Beat 2 egg whites until soft peaks form, gradually add half the caster sugar, beat for a further 3 minutes; fold into chocolate mixture. Pour mousse into 4 large balloon glasses and chill for several hours or until set.
2. To make white chocolate layer, combine white melts with remaining sour cream and remaining egg yolk, stir until smooth. Beat remaining egg whites until soft peaks form, gradually add remaining sugar, beat for a further 3 minutes.
3. Fold into white chocolate mixture and pour on top of chilled milk chocolate mousse, chill to set. Decorate with piped cream and strawberries, dust with cocoa.

Serves 4

tip from the chef

This dessert should be served very cold. If you wish to make a variation, replace the milk chocolate or the white chocolate with bittersweet chocolate.

cointreau
soufflé with syrup

■■□ | Cooking time 20 minutes - Preparation time: 15 minutes

method

1. Beat egg yolks with icing sugar, orange juice and rind until thick and creamy. Beat in the sponge biscuits and Cointreau.
2. Beat egg whites in a separate bowl until soft peaks form. Fold into orange mixture and divide between 4-6 greased and collared, 1/2-cup capacity ramekin dishes. Bake in moderate oven for 15 minutes.
3. To make syrup, combine orange juice, marmalade, lemon juice and sugar in a medium saucepan over moderate heat. Simmer for 5 minutes. Strain through a sieve and serve with soufflés.

Serves 4-6

ingredients

- **4 eggs, separated**
- **1/2 cup icing sugar**
- **1/4 cup orange juice concentrate**
- **grated rind of 1 orange**
- **5 sponge finger biscuits, crumbled**
- **2 tablespoons Cointreau**

syrup

- **1/2 cup freshly squeezed orange juice**
- **1/4 cup orange marmalade**
- **2 tablespoons freshly squeezed lemon juice**
- **1/4 cup caster sugar**

tip from the chef

All soufflés should be served immediately when they are taken out of the oven, as they flatten very quickly.

mocha cream

■□□ | Cooking time: 0 minute - Preparation time: 15 minutes

ingredients

- $1^1/_2$ cups thickened cream
- 1 tablespoon vanilla essence
- 2 teaspoons instant coffee dissolved in 2 teaspoons water
- 100 g/$3^1/_2$ oz dark chocolate, melted
- 3 tablespoons Kahlua or chocolate liqueur
- 4 egg whites
- $^1/_2$ cup caster sugar
- coffee beans to garnish

method

1. Beat cream with vanilla essence and coffee until soft peaks form. Stir in melted chocolate and Kahlua until combined.
2. Whip egg whites until stiff; gradually add sugar and continue to beat until thick and glossy, about 5 minutes.
3. Gently fold meringue into chocolate cream mixture until just combined. Spoon into 4 serving glasses, chill, top with coffee beans to decorate.

Serves 4

tip from the chef

It may be served with chocolate sauce and broken meringue.

raspberries in cointreau with meringue

■□□ | Cooking time: 15 minutes - Preparation time: 20 minutes

method

1. Soak raspberries in orange juice and Cointreau overnight. Drain, reserve syrup. Place raspberries in a single layer over the bottom of a 23 cm/9 in pie dish.
2. Beat egg whites until stiff, gradually add sugar and continue to beat for a further 5 minutes.
3. Spoon or pipe meringue over raspberries, leaving 2 cm/3/4 in to the edge of the dish. Sprinkle icing sugar over the top and bake in moderately low oven for 10 minutes.
4. Meanwhile add brown sugar to reserved syrup and place in a small saucepan over moderate heat, bring to the boil, reduce heat and simmer for 3 minutes. Spoon sauce over berries around edge of dish.

Serves 6

ingredients

- **2 cups raspberries**
- **1 cup freshly squeezed orange juice**
- **3 tablespoons Cointreau**
- **3 egg whites**
- **1/2 cup caster sugar**
- **1 tablespoon icing sugar**
- **1/2 cup brown sugar**

tip from the chef

This is an ideal dessert for Winter time, and tastes delicious with vanilla ice-cream.

snow eggs with rose custard

■■■ | Cooking time: 20 minutes - Preparation time: 20 minutes

method

1. To make crystallized rose petals, brush rose petals with egg white, sprinkle with sugar, place on nonstick baking paper and set aside in a warm place to dry.
2. To make meringues, place egg whites in a bowl and beat until soft peaks form. Continue beating while slowly adding sugar, then beat in lemon juice and beat until soft peaks form.
3. Place milk in a large frying pan and bring to simmering over a medium heat. Using two tablespoons shape spoonfuls of egg white mixture and poach in milk for 2-3 minutes or until cooked. Using a slotted spoon remove meringues from milk and drain on absorbent kitchen paper. Reserve milk.
4. To make custard, place egg yolks and sugar in a heatproof bowl and whisk until thick and creamy. Continue beating while slowly pouring in reserved hot milk. Place bowl over a saucepan of simmering water and cook, stirring constantly, until mixture thickens and coats the back of a metal spoon. Remove bowl from pan and set aside to cool for 5 minutes. Stir yogurt, rose water and raspberry purée into custard mixture. Place bowl in iced water and stir until custard is cold.
5. To serve, divide custard between 4 dessert plates, top with 3 meringues and scatter with rose petals.

Serves 4

ingredients

- **3 egg whites**
- **1 tablespoon caster sugar**
- **1 teaspoon lemon juice**
- **1 cup/250 ml/8 fl oz milk**

rose custard

- **3 egg yolks**
- **2 tablespoons caster sugar**
- **3/4 cup/155 g/5 oz natural yogurt**
- **1 teaspoon rose water**
- **2 tablespoon raspberry purée**

crystallized rose petals

- **12 pink or red rose petals**
- **1 egg white, lightly beaten**
- **2 tablespoons caster sugar**

tip from the chef

To make raspberry purée, place fresh or frozen raspberries in a food processor or blender and process to make a purée, push mixture through a sieve to remove seeds and use as desired.

hazelnut cream meringue

■■□ | Cooking time: 50 minutes - Preparation time: 25 minutes

ingredients

- 6 egg whites
- 1 cup caster sugar
- 2 tablespoons cornflour
- 1 cup ground hazelnuts
- 1 1/4 cups thickened cream
- 2 tablespoons cocoa
- 2 tablespoons icing sugar
- raspberries to serve

sauce

- 3/4 cup thickened cream
- 75 g/2 1/2 oz dark chocolate, grated
- 1/2 cup Nutella (see tip)

method

1. Beat egg whites in a large bowl with an electric mixer until soft peaks form. Gradually add sugar, beat until mixture is thick and glossy. Fold in sifted cornflour and ground hazelnuts (a).
2. Divide mixture between two 22 cm/8 3/4 in paper-lined, greased and floured cake pans (b), spreading mixture evenly over base. Bake in moderately low oven for 45 minutes. Cool cakes for 10 minutes before removing paper and turning onto a wire rack to cool.
3. To make filling, beat cream with cocoa and icing sugar until soft peaks form, spread one meringue with the cream (c), top with other meringue and dust with icing sugar.
4. To make sauce, combine cream, chocolate and Nutella in a small saucepan over low heat, stir constantly (d) until ingredients are combined. Cool slightly and serve with meringue. You may like to serve with fresh raspberries.

Serves 6-8

tip from the chef

Nutella is a commercial brand of choc-hazelnut spread, available in supermarkets.

a

b

c
d

peach crêpes with raspberry sauce

■■□ | Cooking time: 20 minutes - Preparation time: 15 minutes

method

1. Sift flour into a medium bowl, make a well in the center. Combine eggs, butter and milk in a jug, pour into well and slowly mix to a smooth batter. If necessary, blend or process batter to remove any lumps.
2. Pour 2 tablespoons of batter into a heated, greased crêpe pan. Cook until golden on underside, turn crêpe and brown on the other side. Repeat with remaining batter.
3. Heat extra butter in a frying pan over moderate heat, add peach slices, lightly sauté for 1 minute each side, fill each crêpe with peaches, sprinkle with sugar, roll up crêpe.
4. Combine raspberries, Framboise, lemon juice and jam in a medium saucepan over moderate heat, simmer for 5 minutes. Push mixture through a sieve and pour over crêpes to serve.

Serves 6

ingredients

- **3/4 cup plain flour**
- **3 eggs**
- **2 tablespoons melted butter**
- **1 cup milk**
- **30 g/1 oz butter, extra**
- **2 large peaches, peeled and thinly sliced**
- **2 tablespoons caster sugar**
- **1 small box raspberries**
- **2 tablespoons Framboise**
- **1 tablespoon freshly squeezed lemon juice**
- **1/4 cup raspberry jam**

tip from the chef

If you wish to enhance this warm dessert, serve with whipped cream.

apricot layer cake with syrup

■■□ | Cooking time: 50 minutes - Preparation time: 20 minutes

method

1. Sift flour and sugar into a medium bowl; make a well in the center. Stir in combined egg, milk and butter until smooth. You may have to blend or process to remove any lumps.
2. Pour 3 tablespoons of mixture into a heated and greased crêpe pan and cook 1 1/2-2 minutes each side or until golden. Continue until all batter is used.
3. Place a pancake in the base of a greased ovenproof dish. Slice apricot halves into thin slices and toss in the combined caster sugar and cinnamon.
4. Spread a quarter of the apricot mixture on top of the pancake, top with another pancake, then another quarter of the apricot mixture. Repeat this again, ending with a pancake, using in all 5 pancakes. Sprinkle extra caster sugar on top. Bake in moderate oven for 30 minutes.
5. To make syrup, combine 1 cup of the reserved apricot juice with lemon juice, orange rind and apricot jam in a small saucepan over moderate heat. Bring to the boil, reduce heat and simmer for 5 minutes. Serve with pancakes.

Serves 6

ingredients

pancakes

- **1 1/2 cups self-raising flour**
- **2 tablespoons caster sugar**
- **1 egg, lightly beaten**
- **1 1/2 cups milk**
- **30 g/1 oz butter, melted**

filling

- **825 g/1 lb 10 oz canned apricot halves, drained, syrup reserved**
- **1/2 cup caster sugar**
- **1 tablespoon cinnamon**

syrup

- **3 tablespoons freshly squeezed lemon juice**
- **1 tablespoon grated orange rind**
- **2 tablespoons apricot jam**
- **extra caster sugar, to decorate**

tip from the chef

It is also delicious if pears are used instead of apricots.

chocolate fritters

■■■ | Cooking time: 5 minutes - Preparation time: 20 minutes

method

1. Blend or process cake crumbs with cocoa, melted chocolate and cream until smooth. Press mixture over base of a greased and lined loaf tin and freeze for 2 hours.
2. Meanwhile, to make the batter, blend or process flour with custard powder, cinnamon and milk until smooth. Cover and chill until ready to use.
3. Cut chocolate mixture into triangles, dip in batter to coat, deep-fry until golden; drain on absorbent paper.

Makes about 12

ingredients

- **2 cups chocolate cake crumbs**
- **1 tablespoon cocoa**
- **150 g/5 oz dark chocolate, melted**
- **2 tablespoons thickened cream**

batter

- **1/3 cup self-raising flour**
- **1/3 cup custard powder**
- **1/4 teaspoon ground cinnamon**
- **3/4 cup milk**
- **oil for deep-frying**

tip from the chef

In order to obtain a crunchy batter, the oil should be very hot; to check, drop a teaspoon of batter and verify that it turns golden in a few seconds.

plum fritters

■□□ | Cooking time: 5 minutes - Preparation time: 15 minutes

ingredients

- > 1/3 cup self-raising flour
- > 1/3 cup cornflour
- > 1 tablespoon caster sugar
- > 1/2 teaspoon ground cinnamon
- > 3/4 cup milk
- > 16 firm plums
- > oil for deep-frying
- > 1 cup carton custard
- > 1/2 cup thickened cream
- > icing sugar to dust

method

1. Combine flour, cornflour, sugar and cinnamon in a large bowl. Make a well in the center, gradually stir in milk, mix to a smooth batter.
2. Dip plums into batter using a metal skewer, coat well. Deep-fry in a large saucepan of hot oil, 4 at a time, until golden. Drain on absorbent paper.
3. Combine custard and cream in a small bowl, spoon a little custard mixture onto each plate, arrange 3 or 4 plum fritters on the custard. Dust with icing sugar.

Serves 4-6

tip from the chef

It is important that the plums are firm to avoid breaking during cooking.

strawberry feuilleté

■■□ | Cooking time: 20 minutes - Preparation time: 15 minutes

method

1. Cut each sheet of puff pastry in half, then cut each half into 3 rectangles and place on a greased baking tray. Bake in moderately hot oven for 10 minutes; cool on a wire rack.
2. Place half the strawberries, the sugar and lemon juice in a medium saucepan and cook gently over moderately low heat for 10 minutes, stirring constantly. When fruit is soft, push through a sieve and discard pips. Stir kirsch into purée and set aside.
3. Whip cream until light and fluffy, fold in remaining strawberries and spread over 6 of the pastry leaves. Top with remaining 6 leaves, dust with icing sugar and serve in a pool of strawberry purée.

Serves 6

ingredients

- **2 sheets puff pastry**
- **$2\frac{1}{2}$ cups strawberries, hulled and quartered**
- **3 tablespoons sugar**
- **2 tablespoons freshly squeezed lemon juice**
- **1 tablespoon kirsch**
- **2 cups thickened cream**
- **icing sugar to decorate**

tip from the chef

This delicious feuilleté may also be served as a large pie.

miniature cream horns

■□□ | Cooking time: 10 minutes - Preparation time: 15 minutes

ingredients

> 1 sheet puff pastry
> 1 cup thickened cream
> 2 tablespoons icing sugar
> 2 teaspoons cocoa powder
> 1 tablespoon Tia Maria

method

1. Cut pastry sheet into 1 cm/1/2 in thick strips, the length of the pastry. Lightly grease 4 pastry cones. Wrap a strip of pastry around each cone, beginning at the small end, overlapping pastry slightly.
2. Place on a greased baking tray and bake in moderately hot oven for 10 minutes or until golden.
3. Beat cream with icing sugar, cocoa powder and Tia Maria until soft peaks form; chill.
4. Gently ease pastry off cones and cool. When completely cold, pipe cream mixture into pastry cones. Serve immediately.

Makes about 20

tip from the chef

It is an extremely easy recipe, ideal for after dinner talk or tea-time.

peach tart

■■□ | Cooking time: 20 minutes - Preparation time: 20 minutes

method

1. Cut a 23 cm/9 in circle out of one sheet of pastry. Cut remaining sheet into 1 1/2 cm/1/2 in strips. Brush edge of pastry circle with water.
2. Gently press a strip of pastry around the edge of the pastry circle, using fingertips to shape. Continue with remaining strips building up several layers of height as you use all strips.
3. Slice peach halves very finely. Brush pastry base with jam and arrange peaches on top. Brush with melted extra jam and bake in moderate oven for 20 minutes.

Serves 8

ingredients

- **2 sheets puff pastry**
- **2 large peaches, halved, stoned and peeled**
- **1/4 cup peach jam**
- **2 tablespoons peach jam, extra, melted**

tip from the chef

In order to enhance shine, paint the peaches with jam again after taking the pie out of the oven.

chocolate chips pastry pie

■□□ | Cooking time: 15 minutes - Preparation time: 15 minutes

method

1. Cut a 22 cm/8 3/4 in circle from each pastry sheet, brush with egg white, bake on greased baking trays in moderately hot oven for 15 minutes, or until golden. Cool on wire racks.
2. Beat cream with vanilla essence, chocolate and icing sugar until thick.
3. When pastry is cool, sandwich together with the choc-chip cream. Dust top with icing sugar and cocoa.

ingredients

- 3 sheets puff pastry
- 1 egg white
- 2 cups cream
- 1 tablespoon vanilla essence
- 1/2 cup grated dark chocolate
- 1/4 cup icing sugar
- extra icing sugar to dust
- cocoa to dust

Serves 8

tip from the chef

If you wish to make the filling richer, add 1/2 cup of toasted and chopped walnuts.

pear and blackberry pie

■■□ | Cooking time: 30 minutes - Preparation time: 20 minutes

ingredients

- 225 g/7 oz plain flour
- 100 g/3 1/2 oz cold butter, cut into cubes
- 30 g/1 oz caster sugar
- 2-3 tablespoons iced water
- 4 large pears, peeled, cored and sliced
- 3 tablespoons caster sugar
- 2 tablespoons freshly squeezed lemon juice
- 2 cups blackberries
- 2 teaspoons ground cinnamon
- icing sugar to dust

method

1. Combine flour with butter and sugar in a blender or food processor until mixture resembles fine breadcrumbs. Transfer mixture to a bowl and, using a knife, mix in water, quickly knead to bind. Wrap dough and chill for 30 minutes.
2. Place pear slices over the base of a 20 cm/8 in flan dish, sprinkle with sugar, pour over lemon juice. Place berries on top, sprinkle with cinnamon.
3. Roll out pastry, cut out a 20 cm/8 in circle; using a knife, mark out wedges but do not cut right through. Place pastry circle on top of blackberries. Bake in a hot oven for 10 minutes, turn heat to moderate, cook for a further 20 minutes.
4. To serve, cut pastry into wedges. Spoon some of the fruit onto serving plate, top with a wedge of pastry; dust with icing sugar.

Serves 8

tip from the chef

This delicious dessert may be served with champagne sabayon.

summer pudding

■□□ | Cooking time: 5 minutes - Preparation time: 25 minutes

method

1. Remove crusts from bread, cut bread into $1^1/_2$ cm/$^5/_8$ in fingers. Line the base of a 4-cup capacity pudding basin with bread, overlapping slightly; reserve enough for top.
2. Combine berries, sugar, lemon juice and Framboise in a medium saucepan over moderate heat. Bring to the boil, reduce heat and simmer for 5 minutes. Strain syrup from berries, reserving berries and syrup.
3. Pour some of the syrup over the bread, then spoon berries into center. Top with remaining bread, pour over a little more syrup, reserving $^1/_4$ cup for serving.
4. Cover pudding with foil, place a heavy weight on top and refrigerate overnight. To serve, unmold pudding, brush with remaining syrup. Decorate with mint.

Serves 6

ingredients

- **15 slices white bread**
- **750 g/$1^1/_2$ lb berries (boysenberries, blackberries, blueberries)**
- **2 cups caster sugar**
- **2 tablespoons freshly squeezed lemon juice**
- **2 tablespoons Framboise**
- **fresh mint to decorate**

tip from the chef

It is highly suggested to serve this dessert with vanilla ice cream.

bread pudding with dates

■□□ | Cooking time: 40 minutes - Preparation time: 15 minutes

ingredients

- 1 loaf day-old white bread, sliced
- 4 eggs
- 1/2 cup caster sugar
- 2 tablespoons finely grated lemon rind
- 2 cups thickened cream
- 1/2 cup milk
- 1 teaspoon ground cinnamon
- 150 g/5 oz dates, pitted and chopped

method

1. Remove crusts from bread, cut into 1 1/2 cm/5/8 in squares. Beat eggs with sugar until thick. Stir in lemon rind, cream, milk and cinnamon. Stir bread into mixture, mix well and leave to soak for 10 minutes.
2. Stir in dates, pour mixture into a greased ovenproof dish and bake in moderate oven for 35-40 minutes or until cooked through.

Serves 8

tip from the chef

In this extra creamy version of the traditional bread pudding, the raisins are replaced by dates. It may be served with caramel sauce.

high apple pie

■■□ | Cooking time: 1 hour 40 minutes - Preparation time: 35 minutes

method

1. Combine flour, icing sugar and butter in a blender or food processor, process until mixture resembles coarse breadcrumbs; transfer mixture to a large bowl. Add enough cold water to mix to a firm dough.
2. On a lightly floured surface roll out 2/3 pastry, large enough to line the base and slightly overlap side of a 20 cm/8 in springform pan.
3. Place apple slices in a saucepan of water over moderate heat, simmer until just tender; drain and cool to room temperature. Fill pastry case with apples and sultanas, sprinkle with extra sugar, cloves and cinnamon.
4. Roll out remaining pastry, brush edge of pie with egg white, cover with pastry, press edges together and trim.
5. Cut a few slits in pastry top, brush with remaining egg white and sprinkle with caster sugar. Bake in moderate oven for 1 hour; stand 30 minutes before serving.

Serves 6

ingredients

- 2 1/2 cups plain flour
- 1/4 cup icing sugar
- 185 g/6 oz butter, cut into cubes
- 1/3 cup cold water, approx.
- 6 large apples, peeled, cored and sliced
- 1/4 cup sultanas
- 4 tablespoon caster sugar
- 1 teaspoon ground cinnamon
- 1/4 teaspoon ground cloves
- 1 egg white

tip from the chef

It is important to drain the apples well to avoid the dampening of the pastry during the cooking.

index